'. . . no true Democracy has ever existed, nor ever will exist.'

JEAN-JACQUES ROUSSEAU
Born 1712, Geneva, Switzerland
Died 1778, Ermenonville, France

This selection from *Of the Social Contract* (1762) is taken from
Of the Social Contract and Other Political Writings edited by
Chris Bertram and translated by Quintin Hoare,
Penguin Classics, 2012.

ROUSSEAU IN PENGUIN CLASSICS
The Confessions
A Discourse on Inequality
Émile; or, On Education
Of the Social Contract and Other Political Writings
Reveries of the Solitary Walker

JEAN-JACQUES ROUSSEAU

The Body Politic

Translated by
Quintin Hoare

PENGUIN BOOKS

PENGUIN CLASSICS

UK | USA | Canada | Ireland | Australia
India | New Zealand | South Africa

Penguin Classics is part of the Penguin Random House group of companies
whose addresses can be found at global.penguinrandomhouse.com.

Penguin
Random House
UK

This selection first published in Penguin Classics 2016

005

Translation copyright © Quintin Hoare, 2012

The moral right of the translator has been asserted

Set in 10/14.5 pt Baskerville 10 Pro
Typeset by Jouve (UK), Milton Keynes
Printed in Great Britain by Clays Ltd, St Ives plc

A CIP catalogue record for this book is available from the British Library

ISBN: 978–0–241–25201–7

www.greenpenguin.co.uk

MIX
Paper from
responsible sources
FSC® C018179

Penguin Random House is committed to a
sustainable future for our business, our readers
and our planet. This book is made from Forest
Stewardship Council® certified paper.

Contents

OF THE
SOCIAL CONTRACT;
OR,
PRINCIPLES
OF
POLITICAL RIGHT

by J. J. Rousseau,
citizen of Geneva.

. . . foederis aequas
Dicamus leges.
AENEID. XI

Foreword

This little treatise is extracted from a more extensive work, undertaken years ago with no heed for my strength and long since abandoned. Of the various fragments that might be drawn from what was done, this is the most considerable and has seemed to me least unworthy of being presented to the public. The rest already exists no more.

Book I

I wish to explore whether in the civil order – taking men as they are and laws as they can be – there may be any legitimate and reliable rule of administration. In this study, I shall attempt always to ally what is permitted by right to what is prescribed by interest, so that justice and utility may not be divided.

I shall embark upon my theme without first proving the importance of my subject. People will ask if I am a prince or a legislator, to be writing about Politics. I reply that I am not, which is why I am writing about Politics. If I were a prince or legislator, I should not waste my time saying what ought to be done; I should do it, or I should hold my peace.

Since by birth I am a citizen of a free State and a member of its sovereign body, the right to vote on public affairs is enough to impose on me the duty to inform myself about these, however weak an influence upon them my voice may have. Fortunate indeed, whenever I reflect on Governments, always to find in my inquiries new reasons for loving that of my own country!

CHAPTER 1
Subject of This First Book

Man was born free, and everywhere he is in chains. A person deems himself the master of others, yet still remains more of a slave than they. How did this change come about? I do not know. What can make it legitimate? I think I can resolve that question.

If I were to consider force alone and the effect deriving from it, I should say: so long as a People is constrained to obey and obeys, it does well; as soon as it can cast off the yoke and casts it off, it does still better; for, in recovering its liberty by the same right whereby it was robbed of it, either it is entitled to seize back that liberty, or no one was entitled to remove it. But social order is a sacred right, serving as the basis for all others. Yet that right by no means comes from nature; hence, it is founded on conventions. The question is to know what those conventions are. Before tackling this, I must establish what I have just proposed.

CHAPTER 2
Of the First Societies

The oldest of all societies and the only natural one is that of the family. Yet children remain bound to their father only so long as they need him in order to survive. No sooner does this need cease than the natural bond is dissolved. The children released from the obedience they used to owe to their father, the father released from the care he used to owe to his children – all return alike to independence. If they do continue to remain united, this is no longer natural but voluntary, and the family itself is maintained only through convention.

This common liberty is a consequence of man's nature. His first law is to attend to his own survival; his first care is owed to himself and, once he reaches the age of reason, as sole judge of the means appropriate for survival he thereby becomes his own master.

So the family is, if you will, the first model for political societies; the ruler is the image of the father, the people is the image of the children, and all – having been born equal and free – alienate their liberty only where this is useful to them. The sole difference is that in the family a father's love for his children repays him for the care he takes of them, while in the State the pleasure of commanding makes up for that love which the ruler does not have for his people.

Grotius denies that every human power is established in favour of those who are governed, citing the example of slavery. His preferred manner of reasoning is always to establish right by facts.* A more consistent method might be used, but not one more favourable to Tyrants.

Thus, according to Grotius, it is doubtful whether the human race belongs to a hundred men, or whether those hundred men belong to the human race;

---

* 'Scholarly studies on public law are often merely the story of ancient abuses, and people have been over-zealous when they have taken the trouble to pay them too much attention.' *Traité des intérêts de la Fr. avec ses voisins, par M. le Marquis d'Argenson* (printed by Rey in Amsterdam). That is just what Grotius has done. [1782 edition]

throughout his book he seems to lean towards the former opinion – which is also the view of Hobbes. So there we have the human race divided into herds of cattle, each with its ruler who tends it that he may devour it.

Just as a pastor's nature is superior to that of his flock, the shepherds of men – who are their rulers – likewise are of a nature superior to that of their peoples. So reasoned the Emperor Caligula, by Philo's account; fairly concluding from this analogy that kings were Gods, or that peoples were beasts.

Caligula's reasoning is the same as that of Hobbes and Grotius. Before all of them Aristotle too had said that men are by no means naturally equal, but some are born for slavery and others for domination.

Aristotle was right, but he took the effect for the cause. Every man born in slavery is born for slavery, nothing is surer. Slaves lose all in their irons, even the desire to escape them; they love their servitude, just as Ulysses' companions loved their brutish condition.* So if there are slaves by nature, it is because

---

* See a little treatise by Plutarch entitled: 'Beasts are rational' [*Bruta animalia ratione uti*].

there have been slaves against nature. Force made the first slaves, their cowardice has perpetuated them.

I have said nothing about king Adam, nor about Emperor Noah, father of three great Monarchs who divided the universe between them as had Saturn's children, whom some people have thought to recognize in them. I hope that gratitude will be shown me for this moderation. For who knows whether I – descended directly from one of these Princes, and perhaps from the senior branch – might not, if titles were to be verified, find myself legitimate king of the human race? Be that as it may, it cannot be denied that Adam was Sovereign of the world like Robinson of his island, since he was its sole inhabitant; and what was convenient in that empire was that the monarch safe on his throne had nothing to fear from rebellions or wars or conspirators.

CHAPTER 3

Of the Right of the Strongest

The strongest is never strong enough to be forever master, if he does not transform his strength into right and obedience into duty. Whence the right of the strongest: a right in appearance meant ironically, and in reality established as a principle. But will this word ever be explained to us? Strength is a physical power; I cannot at all see what morality can result from its effects. Yielding to force is an act of necessity, not of will; at most it is an act of prudence. In what sense could this be a duty?

Let us assume this supposed right for a moment. I say its only result is an inexplicable muddle. For as soon as it is force that makes right, the effect changes with the cause; any force surmounting the first inherits its right. As soon as you can disobey with impunity, you can do so legitimately; and since the strongest is always right, all that matters is contriving to be strongest. But what right is it, that perishes when strength ceases? If you have to obey by force, you do not need to obey out of duty; and if you are no longer forced to obey, you are no longer obliged to do so. So it is clear that this word 'right' adds nothing to strength; it means nothing at all here.

Obey the powers that be. If that means: yield to force, the precept is good but superfluous: I respond that it will never be violated. Every power comes from God, I admit; but every ailment likewise comes from Him. Does that mean it is forbidden to call the doctor? Let a brigand surprise me in some corner of a wood: not merely must I perforce surrender my purse, but if I could hide it am I in all conscience obliged to hand it over, since the pistol he holds is after all also a power?

Let us agree then that strength does not make right, and that you are obliged to obey only legitimate powers. So my original question still recurs.

CHAPTER 4
Of Slavery

Since no man has a natural authority over his fellow, and since strength produces no right, conventions are left as the basis of every legitimate authority among men.

If an individual, Grotius says, can alienate his liberty and enslave himself to a master, why could not a whole people alienate its own and subject itself to a king? There are plenty of ambiguous words here requiring explanation, but let us confine ourselves to 'alienate'. To alienate is to give or to sell. Now, a man who enslaves himself to another does not give himself, he sells himself, at the very least for his subsistence. But for what does a people sell itself? A king, far from providing his subjects with their subsistence, derives his own subsistence from them alone, and according to Rabelais a king does not live off a pittance. Do subjects then give their person on condition that their property too will be taken? I fail to see what they have left to preserve.

You will say that the despot guarantees civil peace to his subjects. Very well. But what do they gain thereby, if the wars into which his ambition draws them, his insatiable greed, and the humiliations of his rule inflict more desolation upon them than would their own disputes? What do they gain thereby, if that very peace is one of their miseries? One may live at peace even in a dungeon – is that enough to feel at ease there? The Greeks imprisoned in Cyclops' cave lived there peacefully, awaiting their turn to be devoured.

To say that a man gives himself freely is to say something absurd and unthinkable. Such an action is illegitimate and null, if only because the person who performs it is not in his right mind. To say the same thing of an entire people is to assume a people of madmen: madness does not create right.

Even if each man could alienate himself, he cannot alienate his children. They are born men and free; their liberty belongs to them, they alone have the right to dispose of it. Before they have reached the age of reason, their father may in their name stipulate conditions to ensure their survival or their well-being; but not give them away irrevocably and without condition, for such a gift is contrary to the aims of nature and goes beyond the rights of fatherhood. Hence, for an arbitrary government to be legitimate, it would be necessary for the people in each generation to have the power to accept or reject it; but then that government would no longer be arbitrary.

To renounce your liberty is to renounce your character as a man – the rights and even the duties of humanity. There is no possible compensation for someone who renounces everything. Such a renunciation is incompatible with man's nature. To strip his will of all liberty means to strip his actions of all morality. Stipulating on the one hand an absolute authority and on the other a boundless obedience is a vain and contradictory convention. For is it not obvious that you have no obligation to a person from whom you have the right to demand everything? And does not that circumstance – without equivalence, without exchange – of itself nullify the act? For what right could my slave have against me, since all that he has belongs to me; and since, his right being mine, this right of my own against myself has no meaning?

Grotius and others derive from war another source of the so-called right to enslavement. Since, according to them, the victor has the right to slay the vanquished, the latter may purchase his life in return for his liberty; an agreement all the more legitimate in that it benefits both parties.

But it is clear that this supposed right to slay the vanquished in no way results from the state of war. For the simple reason that men living in their primitive independence do not maintain sufficiently constant relations among themselves to constitute either a state of peace or a state of war; they are not natural enemies at all. It is the relationship between things not between men that constitutes war. And since the state of war cannot arise from mere personal relations, but only from property relations, a private war – or war between one man and another – cannot exist, either in the state of nature where there is no constant property, or in the social state where all is governed by laws.

Individual conflicts, encounters or duels are acts that do not constitute a state; and as for the private wars authorized by the legal code of King Louis IX of France and suspended by the Peace of God, they are abuses of feudal government, an absurd system if ever there was one, against the principles of natural law and every good polity.

Thus war is by no means a relationship between one man and another, but a relationship between one State and another, in which individuals are enemies only accidentally, not as men or even as citizens,* but

---

* The Romans, who understood better and respected more the right of war than any other nation in the world, carried their scruples in this respect so far that a Citizen was not allowed to serve as a volunteer without having expressly engaged himself against the enemy, and against the particular enemy by name. When a Legion in which the young Cato was seeing his first service under Popilius was reorganized, Cato the Elder wrote to Popilius that if he wanted his son to continue to serve under him, he must make him swear a new military

as soldiers; not as members of the fatherland, but as its defenders. For any State may have only other States as enemies, not men, considering that no real relation may be fixed between things of differing nature.

This principle even accords with the maxims established in every age and with the constant practice of all civilized peoples. Declarations of war are warnings less to powers than to their subjects. The foreigner – whether king, or individual, or people – who steals from, kills or detains subjects without declaring war upon the prince is not an enemy, he is a brigand. Even in the thick of war, a just prince may indeed seize all that belongs to the public in an enemy country; but he respects the person and the goods of individuals, he respects rights upon which his own are based. Since

---

oath, because the former oath having been annulled he was no longer able to bear arms against the enemy. And that same Cato wrote to his son to take care not to present himself for combat if he had not sworn this new oath. I know that you could bring up against me the siege of Clusium and other specific events, but for my part I am citing laws and customs. The Romans are the people who least often infringed their laws, and they are the only people to have had such fine ones. [1782 edition]

the aim of war is destruction of the hostile State, you have the right to kill its defenders so long as they are bearing arms; but as soon as they lay them down and surrender, ceasing to be enemies or instruments of the enemy, they again become merely men and you no longer have any right over their lives. Sometimes you may kill the State without killing a single one of its members: well, war gives no right that is not necessary to its objective. These principles are not those of Grotius; they are not based on the authority of poets, but derive from the nature of things and are based on reason.

As for the right of conquest, it has no basis other than the law of the strongest. If war does not give the victor the right to massacre the peoples he has vanquished, this right that he does not have cannot be the basis for a right to enslave them. You have the right to kill an enemy only when you cannot make him a slave; thus the right to make him a slave does not come from the right to kill him. It is thus an unjust exchange to make him buy his life, upon which you have no right, at the price of his liberty. In establishing the right of life and death upon the right to enslave, and the right to enslave upon the right of life and death, is it not clear that you are falling into a vicious circle?

Even assuming this dreadful right to kill everyone, I say that a slave made in war – or a conquered people – has no obligation whatsoever towards his master, other than to obey him to the extent that he is forced to do so. By taking an equivalent to his life, the victor has by no means spared it: instead of killing him fruitlessly, he has killed him usefully. Hence, far from the victor having acquired any authority over him in addition to force, the state of war subsists between them as before, their very relationship is a consequence of it, and use of the right of war implies no peace treaty. They have made a convention, very well; but that convention, far from destroying the state of war, implies its continuation.

Thus, however you look at things, the right to enslave is non-existent, not just because it is illegitimate, but because it is absurd and means nothing. The words *slavery* and *right* are contradictory; they mutually exclude one another. Whether from a man to a man, or from a man to a people, this argument will always be equally preposterous: *I make a convention with you entirely at your expense and entirely for my benefit, which I shall observe to whatever extent pleases me, and which you will observe to whatever extent pleases me.*

CHAPTER 5
*How It Is Always Necessary to
Go Back to a Primary Pact*

Even were I to accept all that I have hitherto rejected, the advocates of despotism would thereby be no further forward. There will always be a great difference between subduing a multitude and governing a society. In the fact that dispersed men may successively have been enslaved – in whatever numbers – to a single individual, I perceive only a master and slaves, and by no means a people and its ruler. It is an aggregation, if you will, but not an association; neither public good nor body politic is involved here. Had that man enslaved half the world, he is still just an individual; his interest, separated from that of other men, is still just a private interest. If this same man happens to perish, his empire after him is left dispersed and disconnected, just as an oak dissolves and falls in a heap of ashes once the fire has consumed it.

A people, Grotius says, can give itself to a king. According to Grotius, therefore, a people is a people before giving itself to a king. This very gift is a civil act, assuming some public deliberation. So before examining the act whereby a people elects a king, it would be useful to examine the act by virtue of which a people is a people. For since this latter act necessarily precedes the former, it is the true foundation of society.

If there were no prior convention, in fact, where would be the obligation for the minority – unless the election were unanimous – to submit to the choice of the majority? And whence do a hundred who wish for a master have the right to vote for ten who do not wish for one at all? The law of voting by plurality is itself established by convention, and assumes unanimity on at least one occasion.

CHAPTER 6
Of the Social Pact

I assume men arrived at the point where the obstacles impeding their preservation in a state of nature prevail, through their resistance, over the forces each individual can deploy to maintain himself in such a state. The primitive state can then no longer subsist, and mankind would perish if it did not change its way of being.

Now, since men cannot engender new forces, but merely unite and direct those that exist, they no longer have any means of self-preservation other than to form by aggregation a sum of forces capable of overcoming the resistance, to bring these into play through a single motive force, and to make them act in concert.

This sum of forces can be born only from the cooperation of many: but since the strength and liberty of each man are the first instruments of his preservation, how shall he commit them without harming himself, without neglecting the care he owes to himself? In relation to my subject, this difficulty can be articulated in the following terms. *How to find a form of association that will, with the whole common force, defend and protect the person and goods of each associate, and through which each individual, while uniting with all, will nevertheless obey himself alone and remain as free as before?* Such is the fundamental problem to which the social contract gives the solution.

The clauses of this contract are so much determined by the nature of the act that the least modification would render them vain and ineffective; so that, although they have perhaps never been formally articulated, they are everywhere the same, everywhere tacitly accepted and recognized; until such time as the social pact has been violated, when each person is restored to his original rights and recovers his natural liberty, losing the liberty by compact for which he renounced the latter.

These clauses can all be reduced, of course, to one alone: namely, the total alienation of each associate with all his rights to the community as a whole. For initially, since each person surrenders himself entirely, the condition is equal for all; and since the condition is equal for all, no one has any interest in making it onerous for the rest.

Moreover, since the alienation is made without reservation, the union is as perfect as may be, and no associate has anything further to claim. For if individuals did retain some rights, there would be no common superior able to adjudicate between them and the public. Then everyone, being his own judge on certain matters, would soon claim to be his own judge on all. The state of nature would thus live on, and the association would necessarily become tyrannical or vain.

For since each person gives himself to all, he gives himself to no one. And since there is no associate over whom you do not acquire the same right that you grant him over yourself, you gain the equivalent of all that you lose, and more strength to preserve what you have.

So if you eliminate from the social pact what is not essential to it, you will find it is reduced to the following terms. *Each of us places his person and all his power in common under the supreme direction of the general will; and as a body we receive each member as an indivisible part of the whole.*

Instantly, in place of the particular person of each contracting party, this act of association produces a corporate and collective body composed of as many members as the assembly has votes: a body that receives from this very act its unity, its common *self*, its life and its will. This public person thus formed by the union of all the rest was formerly given the name of *City*,* and is now given the name of *Republic* or *body politic*; which is called a *State* by its members when it is passive, a *Sovereign* when it is active, a *Power* when comparing it with its likes. So far as the associates are concerned, they collectively take the name of *people*, and in particular are called *Citizens* as participants in the sovereign authority, and *Subjects* as

---

*   The true meaning of this word has been almost wholly erased in the modern world; most people today take a town for a City and a townsman for a Citizen. They are unaware that houses make a town but Citizens make a City. This same mistake once cost the Carthaginians dear. I have not read that the title *Cives* has ever been given to the subjects of any Prince, not even in olden times to the Macedonians, nor in our own day to the English, closer to liberty though they be than all the rest. The French alone adopt this title of *Citizens* quite casually, since as can be seen from their Dictionaries they have no real idea about it; otherwise by usurping it they would fall into the crime of Lèse-Majesté. Among them, this name expresses a quality, not a right. When Bodin thought to speak about our Citizens and Townsmen, he made a serious blunder in taking one for the other. M. d'Alembert did not fall into the same error, and in his article 'Geneva' clearly distinguished the four orders of men (even five, counting mere foreigners) who exist in our town, and of whom two alone make up the Republic. No other French author, to my knowledge, has understood the true meaning of the word *Citizen*.

subjugated to the laws of the State. But these terms are often confused and taken one for the other; it is enough to know how to distinguish them when they are used with full precision.

CHAPTER 7
Of the Sovereign

It is clear from this formula that the act of association involves a reciprocal engagement between private persons and the public. And that each individual, contracting so to speak with himself, finds himself engaged by a twofold relationship: namely, as a member of the Sovereign towards private persons, and as a member of the State towards the Sovereign. But you cannot here apply the maxim of civil right that no one is bound by engagements to himself; for there is a clear difference between incurring an obligation to yourself and incurring one to a whole of which you form part.

We must further note that public deliberation, which may involve all subjects in an obligation towards the Sovereign, thanks to the two different relations in terms of which each of them is viewed, cannot for the opposite reason involve the Sovereign in an obligation towards itself; and that it is thus against the nature of the body politic for the Sovereign to impose a law on itself that it could not infringe. Being unable to consider itself other than in terms of one single relation, it is thus in the same situation as a private person contracting with himself. From which it may be seen that there is not – and cannot be – any kind of fundamental law binding on the body of the people, not even the social contract. Which does not mean that this body cannot perfectly well engage itself to others in whatever does not infringe this contract; for in relation to foreigners it becomes a simple being, an individual.

But the body politic or Sovereign, drawing its being solely from the sanctity of the contract, can never incur an obligation – even towards another – for anything that infringes that primitive act, such as alienating some part of itself or submitting itself to another Sovereign. Violating the act whereby it exists would mean annihilating itself, and that which is nothing produces nothing.

As soon as the multitude is thus assembled into a

body, you cannot harm one of its members without attacking the body; still less harm the body without the members feeling the effect. Thus duty and interest alike oblige the two contracting parties to help one another mutually, and the same men must seek to combine in this twofold relationship all the advantages flowing from it.

Now the Sovereign, being formed only by the individuals who make it up, neither has nor can have any interest contrary to theirs; hence, the Sovereign power has no need of a guarantor against its subjects, since it is impossible that the body should wish to harm all its members, and we shall see later that it cannot harm anyone individually. The Sovereign, merely by virtue of its existence, is always all that it must be.

But the same is not true for subjects against the Sovereign, to which despite the common interest nothing would guarantee their commitments, if it did not find means to ensure their loyalty.

Every individual may indeed as a man have a particular will contrary or dissimilar to the general will that he has as a Citizen. His particular interest can speak to him quite otherwise than the general will.

His absolute and naturally independent existence can make him see what he owes to the common cause as a gratuitous contribution, the loss of which will be less harmful to others than payment of it is burdensome to himself. And viewing the corporate person which constitutes the State as a fictive being, since it is not a man, he would enjoy the rights of a citizen without wishing to fulfil the duties of a subject: an injustice that if it persisted would cause the ruin of the body politic.

Thus, in order that the social pact should not be a vain formula, it tacitly incorporates a commitment that alone can give force to the rest: namely, that whosoever refuses to obey the general will shall be constrained to do so by the entire body. This means nothing other than that he shall be forced to be free. For such is the condition that, by giving each Citizen to the Fatherland, guarantees him against all personal dependence: the condition that makes the artifice and play of the political machinery, and that alone gives legitimacy to civil engagements which without it would be absurd, tyrannical and subject to the most enormous abuses.

CHAPTER 8
Of the Civil State

This passage from the state of nature to the civil state produces a most remarkable change in man, by substituting justice for instinct in his behaviour and endowing his actions with the morality they previously lacked. Only then, when the voice of duty succeeds physical impulsion and law succeeds appetite, does man, who until now had thought only of himself, find himself forced to act according to other principles, and to consult his reason before heeding his inclinations. Although in this state he denies himself a number of advantages granted him by nature, he gains others so great in return – his faculties are exercised and developed, his ideas expanded, his feelings ennobled, his entire soul soars so high – that if the abuses of this new condition did not often degrade him below that from which he emerged, he ought continually to bless the happy moment that wrested him thence for ever, and out of a stupid, limited animal made an intelligent being and a man.

Let us reduce this whole balance to terms easily

compared. What man loses through the social contract is his natural liberty, and a limitless right to all that tempts him and that he can reach. What he wins is civil liberty and ownership of all that he possesses. In order not to be mistaken about these compensations, a clear distinction must be made between natural liberty, which has no limits other than the powers of the individual, and civil liberty, which is limited by the general will; between possession, which is the result merely of force or the right of the first occupant, and property, which can be based only on a positive title.

Apart from the foregoing, to the gains of the civil state might be added moral liberty, which alone makes man truly master of himself; for the impulsion of mere appetite is slavery, while obedience to the law you have set yourself is liberty. But I have said too much already on this topic, and the philosophical meaning of the word 'liberty' is not my subject here.

CHAPTER 9
Of Real Estate

Each member of the community gives himself to it at the moment of its formation, just as he currently is: himself and all his powers, including the goods he possesses. It is not that by this act possession changes its nature in changing hands, and becomes property in the hands of the Sovereign. But since the powers of the City are incomparably greater than those of an individual, public possession in fact is also stronger and more irrevocable, without being more legitimate, at least for foreigners. For the State with respect to its members is master of all their goods through the social contract, which in the State serves as the basis for all rights; but with respect to other Powers it is master only through the right of the first occupant, which it derives from individuals.

The right of the first occupant, though more real than that of the strongest, becomes a true right only after establishment of the right of property. Every man naturally has a right to all that is necessary to him; but the positive act that makes him the owner of some good excludes him from all the rest. Once his share is allotted he must limit himself to that, and no longer has any right to common property. This is why the right of the first occupant, so weak in the state of nature, is respected by every civil man. What is respected in this right is less what belongs to another than what does not belong to you.

In general, in order to authorize the right of the first occupant over any piece of land, the following conditions are necessary. First, that this land not yet be occupied by anyone; secondly, that you occupy only so much of it as you need to subsist; in the third place, that you take possession of it not through some vain ceremony, but by labour and cultivation, the only sign of ownership that, in the absence of legal titles, should be respected by others.

For if you grant the right of first occupant to need and to labour, are you not extending that right as far as it will go? Is it possible to place no limits upon it? Will it be enough to set foot on a piece of common land, in order at once to claim you are master of it? Will it be enough to have the strength to keep other men out of it for a while, in order to deny them the right ever to return to it? How can a man or a people seize hold of an immense territory and deprive the entire human race of it, other than through a usurpation deserving of punishment, since it denies to all other men the residence and sustenance that nature gives them in common? When Nuñez Balboa on the coast took possession of the South Sea and all southern America in the name of the crown of Castile, was that enough to dispossess all its inhabitants and exclude from it all the Princes of the world? If such were the case, those ceremonies were multiplied to no purpose, and the Catholic King had only to take possession of the entire universe at a stroke from his study, subject to later subtracting from his empire what was already possessed by other Princes.

How the combined and contiguous lands of individuals become public territory is easily understood, and how the right of sovereignty, extending from the subjects to the land they occupy, becomes at once real and personal; which places the possessors in a greater dependence and makes their very forces into guarantees of their loyalty. An advantage that seems not to have been appreciated by the monarchs of old, who in calling themselves simply kings of the

Persians, Scythians or Macedonians appeared to see themselves as rulers of men rather than masters of a country. Their counterparts today more astutely call themselves Kings of France, Spain, England, etc. By thus holding the land, they are quite sure of holding its inhabitants.

What is singular about this alienation is that the community, far from despoiling individuals of their goods when it accepts these, only ensures their legitimate possession of them, changing usurpation into a genuine right, use into ownership. Thus, with the possessors being considered as trustees of the public good, their rights respected by all members of the State and upheld with all the latter's powers against foreigners, they have in a manner of speaking, through a transfer advantageous both to the public and still more to themselves, gained all that they have given. A paradox easily explained by the distinction between the rights the sovereign and the proprietor have to the same land, as we shall see later.

It may also happen that men begin to unite before they possess anything, and that later, seizing enough land for all of them, they use this in common or share it among themselves, either equally or according to proportions established by the Sovereign. In whatever way this acquisition is made, the right that each individual has over his own land is always subordinated to the right that the community has over all, without which there would be neither solidity in the social bond, nor real force in the exercise of Sovereignty.

I shall end this chapter and this book by a remark that should serve as the basis for the whole social system. It is that, rather than destroying natural equality, the fundamental pact on the contrary substitutes a corporate and legitimate equality for whatever physical inequality nature may have placed among men; and that, whereas they may be unequal in strength or intelligence, they all become equal through convention and by right.*

End of the First Book

---

* Under bad governments this equality is only apparent and illusory; it serves only to maintain the poor man in his misery and the rich man in his usurpation. In fact, laws are always useful to those who own and harmful to those who have nothing. Whence it follows that the social state is advantageous to men only in so far as all have something and none has anything in excess.

Book III

Before speaking about the different forms of Government, let us attempt to fix the precise meaning of this word, which has not yet been very well explained.

CHAPTER 1
Of Government in General

I warn the reader that this chapter must be read carefully, and that I do not have the trick of being clear to anyone who is not willing to be attentive.

Every free action has two causes that contribute to producing it: one moral, namely the will that determines the act; the other physical, namely the power that executes it. When I walk towards an object, it is necessary first that I should wish to go there; in the second place that my feet should carry me there. If a paralytic should wish to run or a nimble man not wish to do so, both will remain where they are. The body politic has the same motive forces. Strength and will are similarly to be discerned there: the latter designated as 'legislative power', the former as 'executive power'. Nothing is done there, nor must be, without their contribution.

We have seen how legislative power belongs to the people, and can belong to the people alone. On the other hand, it is easy to see by the principles established above that executive power cannot belong to the general public, as Legislative or Sovereign. For this power consists only in particular acts that are not the province of law, nor consequently of the Sovereign, all of whose acts can only be laws. Hence, public force needs a specific agent to unite and actuate it as directed by the general will; to enable the State and the Sovereign to communicate; to do in the public realm, in a way, what the union of soul and body does in man. This is the reason for Government in the State, improperly confused with the Sovereign of which it is only the minister.

So what is Government? An intermediary body established between the subjects and the Sovereign for their mutual correspondence, charged with the execution of laws and with the maintenance of liberty, both civil and political.

The members of this body are called Magistrates or *Kings*, in other words *Governors*, and the whole body bears the name of *Prince*.* Hence, those who claim that the act whereby a people submits to rulers is no contract are perfectly correct. This act is nothing whatsoever but a commission; a task in which, as mere officers of the Sovereign, they exercise in the latter's name the power that it has vested in them; a power that it can limit, modify and take back when it likes, the alienation of such a right being incompatible with the nature of the social body and contrary to the purpose of association.

Thus I call *Government* or supreme administration the legitimate exercise of executive power, and Prince or magistrate the man or body charged with this administration.

It is in Government that the intermediate forces are to be found whose relations constitute the relationship

---

*   Thus in Venice the College is called *most serene Prince*, even when the Doge is not present.

between the whole and the whole, or between the Sovereign and the State. This latter relationship can be represented as the ratio between the extremes of a continued proportion of which the mean proportional is the Government. The Government receives from the Sovereign the orders that it gives to the people, and for the State to be well balanced there must, all things being equal, be parity between the product or power of the Government taken in itself and the product or power of the citizens, who are sovereign on the one hand and subjects on the other.

Moreover, it would not be possible to alter any one of the three terms without instantly destroying the proportion. If the Sovereign wishes to govern, or if the magistrate wishes to give laws, or if the subjects refuse to obey, disorder succeeds rule, force and will no longer act in concert, and the dissolved State thus falls into despotism or into anarchy. For as there is only one mean proportional within each ratio, there is likewise only one possible good government in a State. But as a thousand events may change a people's relations, diverse Governments can be good not merely for different peoples, but for the same people at different times.

In an attempt to give an idea of the diverse relations

that can obtain between these two extremes, I shall take as an example the number of the people, this being an easier ratio to express.

Let us suppose that the State is composed of ten thousand Citizens. The Sovereign can be considered only collectively and as a body. But each particular man as a subject is considered as an individual. Thus the Sovereign is to the subject as ten thousand is to one. In other words, each member of the State has for his own share only one ten-thousandth part of the sovereign authority, even though he is wholly subjected to it. If the people consists of one hundred thousand men, the state of the subjects does not change, and each one bears equally the full empire of the laws, while his suffrage, reduced to one hundred-thousandth, has ten times less influence in their drafting. Hence, the subject always remaining single, the ratio between subject and Sovereign increases in proportion to the number of Citizens. Whence it follows that the more the State is enlarged, the more liberty is diminished.

When I say that the ratio increases, I mean that it moves further from parity. So the larger the ratio in the Geometers' sense, the smaller it is in the everyday sense. In the former the ratio, considered in terms of quantity, is measured by the quotient; whereas in the latter, considered in terms of identity, it is gauged by similarity.

Well, the less that particular wills relate to the general will, or morals to laws, the more that repressive force must increase. So the Government, in order to be good, must be relatively stronger to the extent that the people is more numerous.

On the other hand, since enlargement of the State gives those in whom public authority is vested more temptations and means to abuse their power, the more strength the Government must have to contain the people, the more the Sovereign must have in turn in order to contain the Government. I am speaking here not about an absolute strength, but about the relative strength of the different parts of the State.

It follows from this double ratio that the continued proportion between the Sovereign, the Prince and the people is by no means an arbitrary idea, but a necessary consequence of the nature of the body politic. It further follows that since one of the extremes, namely the people as subject, is fixed and represented by unity, whenever the duplicate ratio increases or diminishes, the simple ratio increases or diminishes likewise; and that consequently the middle term is changed. This shows that there is no unique and absolute constitution of Government, but that there can be as many Governments different in nature as States different in size.

If you were to ridicule this system by saying that, in order to find this mean proportional and form the body of Government, all that is necessary according to me is to find the square root of the number of the people, I should reply that I am taking this number here only as an example; that the relations about which I am speaking are measured not merely by the number of men, but in general by the quantity of action, which is the product of innumerable causes; and that furthermore, if in order to express myself in fewer words I borrow for a moment from geometrical terms, I am nevertheless not unaware that geometrical precision has no place in moral quantities.

The Government is in miniature what the body politic encompassing it is on a large scale. It is a corporate person endowed with certain faculties, active like the Sovereign, passive like the State; a person that can be broken down into other similar relations, which accordingly give birth to a new proportion, and within this yet another in accordance with the order of magistracies, until an indivisible middle term is reached, viz. a single head or supreme magistrate, who can be represented in the middle of this progression like the unity between the series of fractions and the series of integers.

Without entangling ourselves in this multiplication of terms, let us content ourselves with considering the Government as a new body in the State, distinct from the people and from the Sovereign, and intermediary between one and the other.

There is this essential difference between these two bodies, that the State exists by virtue of itself, while the Government exists only by virtue of the Sovereign. Thus the dominant will of the Prince is or must be only the general will or the law, and its force is only the public force concentrated in it; no sooner does it seek to perform some absolute and independent act of its own accord than the cohesion of the whole begins to loosen. If it happened indeed that the Prince had an individual will more active than that of the Sovereign, and that in obedience to this individual will it made use of the public force which is in its hands so that in a manner of speaking you had two sovereigns, one de jure and one de facto, the social union would instantly vanish and the body politic would be dissolved.

However, in order for the body of the Government to have an existence, a real life distinguishing it from the body of the State, and in order for all its members to be able to act in concert and answer the purpose for which it is established, it needs an individual *self*, a sensibility common to its members, a force and will of its own directed at its preservation. This individual existence presupposes assemblies, councils, a power of deliberation and resolution; rights, titles and privileges that belong to the Prince exclusively and make the condition of the magistrate proportionately more honourable the more burdensome it is. The difficulties lie in the manner of ordering within the whole this subaltern whole, in such a way that it does not at all alter the general constitution by asserting its own; that it always distinguishes its individual force, destined for its own preservation, from the public force destined for preservation of the State; and that, in a word, it is always ready to sacrifice the Government to the people and not the people to the Government.

Moreover, although the artificial body of the

Government is the work of another artificial body and has in a sense only a borrowed and subordinate life, that does not prevent it from being able to act with more or less vigour or celerity; from so to speak enjoying more or less sound health. For, without departing directly from the purpose of its establishment, it may diverge from it more or less according to the way in which it is constituted.

It is all these differences that give rise to the diverse relations that the Government must have with the body of the State, in keeping with the accidental and particular relations by which this same State is modified. For often the best Government in itself will become the most vice-ridden, if its relations are not altered in accordance with the failings of the body politic to which it belongs.

CHAPTER 2

*Of the Principle That Constitutes
the Diverse Forms of Government*

In order to uncover the general cause of these differences, it is necessary here to distinguish between the

Prince and the Government, as I distinguished above between the State and the Sovereign.

The magistracy can be made up of a greater or lesser number of members. We have already said that the ratio between Sovereign and subjects was greater insofar as the people was more numerous; and by an obvious analogy we can say the same about the Government with respect to the Magistrates.

Now the total force of the Government, being always that of the State, does not vary. Whence it follows that the more it uses this force upon its own members, the less it has left to act upon all the people.

Thus the more numerous the Magistrates, the weaker the Government. Since this maxim is fundamental, let us set about clarifying it.

We can distinguish in the person of the magistrate three essentially different wills. Firstly, the individual's own will, directed only at his private advantage; secondly, the common will of the magistrates, which relates solely to the advantage of the Prince and can be called corporate will, general with respect to the Government and particular with respect to the State of which the Government forms part; in the third place, the will of the people or sovereign will, which

47

is general with respect to the State considered as the whole and likewise to the Government considered as part of the whole.

In a perfect legislation, the particular or individual will must be nil; the corporate will proper to the Government must be very subordinate; hence, the general or sovereign will must be always dominant, and the sole rule for all the others.

According to the natural order, on the other hand, these different wills become proportionately more active the more concentrated they are. Thus the general will is always the weakest, the corporate will ranks second, and the particular will is foremost: so that in Government each member is primarily himself, then a Magistrate, then a citizen. A gradation directly contrary to that required by the social order.

Given this, suppose all Government to be in the hands of a single man. You thus have the particular will perfectly joined with the corporate will, and the latter consequently at the highest degree of intensity attainable. Now, since it is upon the degree of will that the use of force depends, and since the absolute force of the Government is invariable, it follows that the most active of Governments is that of a single man.

On the other hand, let us unite Government with legislative authority. Let us make the Sovereign into the Prince, and all the Citizens into so many magistrates. Then the corporate will, merged into the general will, shall have no more activity than the latter, and leave the particular will in all its force. Hence the Government, still with the same absolute force, will be at its *minimum* of relative force or activity.

These ratios are incontestable, and other considerations serve to confirm them further. Each magistrate, for example, is seen to be more active in his body than each citizen in his, and as a consequence the particular will has much more influence upon the Government's acts than upon the Sovereign's. For each magistrate is almost always charged with some function of Government, whereas each citizen taken separately has no function of sovereignty. Moreover, the more the State expands, the more its real force increases, although it does not increase in proportion to its size. But with the State remaining the same, the magistrates multiply to no avail; the Government does not thereby acquire a greater real force, since this force is that of the State and its measure is always equal. Hence, the relative force or the activity of the Government diminishes, without its absolute or real force being able to increase.

It is certain, moreover, that business is dispatched more slowly, the more people are charged with it; that, in according too much to prudence, not enough is accorded to fortune; that opportunities are let slip; and that, by dint of deliberating, the fruit of deliberation is often lost.

I have just proved that Government slackens to the extent that magistrates multiply, and I proved earlier that the more numerous a people is, the more repressive force must increase. Whence it follows that the ratio between magistrates and Government must be the inverse of the ratio between subjects and Sovereign. In other words, the more the State grows in size, the more the Government must be restricted, in such a way that the number of rulers diminishes proportionately with the people's increase.

However, I am speaking here about the relative force of the Government, not about its rectitude. For, on the contrary, the more numerous the magistracy, the more closely its corporate will approaches the general will. Whereas, as I have said, under a single magistrate that same corporate will is merely a particular will. Thus you lose on one side what you may gain on the other, and the Legislator's art is to succeed in fixing the point at which the Government's force and will, always in reciprocal proportion, combine in the ratio most advantageous to the State.

CHAPTER 3

Division of Governments

It has been seen in the preceding chapter why the various kinds or forms of Government are distinguished by the number of members composing them. It remains to be seen in this chapter how this division is made.

The Sovereign, in the first place, can entrust the charge of Government to the whole people or to the greater part of the people, in such a way that there are more citizens who are magistrates than are simple private citizens. This form of Government is given the name of *Democracy*.

Or it can confine Government within the hands of a small number, in such a way that there are more simple private Citizens than magistrates, and this form bears the name of *Aristocracy*.

Finally it can concentrate the whole Government in the hands of a single magistrate, from whom all the rest hold their power. This third form is the most common, and is called *Monarchy* or royal Government.

It must be noted that all these forms, or at least the two first, are capable of more or less, and have even a fairly broad scope. For Democracy can encompass the whole people or be restricted to half. Aristocracy, in turn, from half the people can be restricted without specification to the smallest number. Even Royalty is capable of being shared to some extent. Sparta always had two Kings according to its constitution; and in the Roman Empire eight Emperors were seen at one time without it being possible to say that the Empire was divided. Thus there is a point at which each form of Government merges with the next and, under just three designations, Government is in reality seen to be capable of as many diverse forms as the State has Citizens.

That is not all. Since this same Government is able in certain respects to be subdivided into different parts, one administered in one way and another in a different way, these three forms in combination can produce a multitude of mixed forms, each of which is multipliable by all the simple forms.

Throughout time, people have always argued a lot about the best form of Government, without considering that every such form is best in certain cases and worst in others.

If in different States the number of supreme magistrates must be in inverse ratio to the number of Citizens, it follows that in general Democratic Government suits small states, the Aristocratic form middling ones, and the Monarchical form large ones. This rule is drawn directly from the principle. But how are we to count the multitude of circumstances that can furnish exceptions?

CHAPTER 4
Of Democracy

He who makes the law knows better than anyone how it should be executed and interpreted. So you could seemingly not have a better constitution than one in which executive power and legislative power were joined. But this is precisely what makes this form of Government inadequate in certain respects, because things that ought to be distinguished are not; the Prince and the Sovereign being merely the same person, they form so to speak merely a Government without Government.

It is not good that he who makes the laws should execute them, nor that the body of the people should turn its attention from general considerations in order to direct it at particular objects. Nothing is more dangerous than the influence of private interests in public affairs, and abuse of the laws by Government is a lesser evil than corruption of the Legislator, inevitable consequence of particular considerations. The substance of the State being then adulterated, every reform becomes impossible. A people that would never abuse Government would not abuse independence either; a people that would always govern well would have no need to be governed.

Taking the term in its strictest sense, no true Democracy has ever existed, nor ever will exist. It is against the natural order for the large number to govern and the small to be governed. One cannot imagine the people remaining constantly assembled to attend to public affairs, and can easily see that it would not be able to establish commissions for this purpose without the form of administration changing.

Indeed, I think I can lay down as a principle that when the functions of Government are shared among several tribunals, the less numerous sooner or later acquire the greatest authority; if only because their facility in dispatching business leads them naturally to acquire it.

Furthermore, how many things does this Government [Democracy] not presuppose that are hard to combine? In the first place a very small State, in which the people is easy to assemble and in which every citizen can easily know all the rest. Secondly, a great simplicity of mores, to avert proliferating business and thorny discussions. Next considerable equality of rank and fortune, without which equality could not long subsist in rights and authority. Lastly little or no luxury, for either luxury is the result of wealth or it makes wealth necessary; it corrupts the rich man and the poor man alike, the former by possession and the latter by envy; it sells the fatherland to softness and vanity; it strips the State of all its Citizens in order to enslave them to each other, and all to public opinion.

That is why a celebrated author gave to the Republic virtue as its principle. For all these conditions could not subsist without virtue. But without having made the necessary distinctions, that fine genius often lacked aptness and sometimes clarity; he did not see that, Sovereign authority being everywhere the same, the same principle must apply in every well-constituted State, more or less to be sure depending on the form of Government.

Let us add that there is no Government so subject to civil war and internal strife as the Democratic or popular kind, because there is none that tends so strongly and continually to change form, nor that requires more vigilance and courage in order to be maintained in its own. It is above all in this constitution that the Citizen must arm himself with force and constancy, and each day of his life say in his innermost heart what a virtuous Palatine* used to

---

* The Palatine of Poznan, father of the King of Poland, Duke of Lorraine.

say in the Polish Diet: *Malo periculosam libertatem quem quietum servitium.*

If there were a people of Gods, it would govern itself Democratically. So perfect a Government is not suitable for men.

CHAPTER 5
Of Aristocracy

We have here two quite distinct corporate persons [*personnes morales*], viz. the Government and the Sovereign, and consequently two general wills, one relative to all citizens, the other only for members of the administration. Hence, although the Government can regulate its internal order as it pleases, it can only ever speak to the people in the name of the Sovereign, viz. in the name of the people itself, and this must never be forgotten.

The first societies were governed aristocratically. The heads of families would deliberate on public affairs among themselves. Young people would yield readily to the authority of experience. Whence such terms as Priests, elders, senate, Gerontes. The natives of North

America still govern themselves thus today, and are very well governed.

But as institutional inequality prevailed over natural inequality, wealth or power* was preferred to age, and Aristocracy became elective. Finally power, transmitted with the father's goods to the children, by making families patrician made Government hereditary, and Senators of twenty were seen.

So there are three kinds of Aristocracy: natural, elective and hereditary. The first suits only simple peoples; the third is the worst of all Governments. The second is the best: it is Aristocracy in the proper sense.

Apart from the advantage of the two powers being distinguished, it has that of its members being chosen. For in a popular Government all Citizens are born as magistrates, but this system limits them to a small number, and they become so only through election;† a means through which probity,

---

* Clearly the word *Optimists* in the ancient world does not mean the best, but the most powerful.

† It is of great importance to regulate the form of elections of magistrates by laws. For if it is left to the will of the Prince, you cannot avoid falling into hereditary Aristocracy, as

enlightenment, experience and all the other reasons for preference and public esteem are so many new guarantees that you will be governed wisely.

Moreover, assemblies are convened more easily, business is discussed better and dispatched in a more orderly and diligent fashion, the credit of the State is upheld better among foreigners by venerable senators than by an unknown or despised multitude.

In a word, the best and most natural order is that the wisest should govern the multitude, when you are sure that they will govern it for its own benefit rather than for theirs. Competencies should not be multiplied needlessly, nor should you do with twenty thousand men what one hundred chosen men can do still better. But it must be noted that corporate interest begins to direct the public force less in keeping with the general will here, and that another inevitable tendency removes part of the executive power from the laws.

happened to the Republics of Venice and Berne. Thus the former has for long been a dissolved State, but the latter maintains itself through the extreme wisdom of its Senate; it is a very honourable and very dangerous exception.

With respect to particular interests, you need neither a State so small nor a people so simple and upright that execution of the laws follows immediately from the public will, as in a good Democracy. Nor do you need a nation so large that the rulers dispersed to govern it ape the Sovereign, each in his own department, and begin by making themselves independent only to end up becoming the masters.

But if Aristocracy requires a few virtues less than popular Government, it also requires others that are specific to it; like moderation among the wealthy and contentment among the poor; for a strict equality would seemingly be out of place in it and was not observed even in Sparta.

Moreover, if this form involves a certain inequality of fortune, this is in order that in general the administration of public business should be entrusted to those who can best give all their time to it; but not, as Aristotle claims, in order that the wealthy should always be preferred. On the contrary, it is important that an opposite choice should sometimes teach the people that in the merit of men there are more important reasons for preference than wealth.

CHAPTER 6
Of Monarchy

Hitherto we have considered the Prince as a corporate [*morale*] and collective person, united by the force of the laws and vested with executive power in the State. Now we have to consider such power concentrated in the hands of a natural person, a real man, who alone has the right to dispense it in keeping with the laws. This is what is called a Monarch, or a King.

Quite unlike other administrations, where a collective being represents an individual, here an individual represents a collective being. So that the corporate unity constituting the Prince is at the same time a physical unity, in which all the faculties that the law so laboriously assembles in the former here find themselves assembled naturally.

Thus the will of the people and the will of the Prince and the public force of the State and the particular force of the Government all respond to the same motive force; all the levers of the machine are in the same hand; everything moves towards the same end; there are no contrary movements mutually destroying one another; and no kind of constitution is imaginable in which a lesser effort would produce a more considerable action. Archimedes seated tranquilly on the shore and effortlessly launching a large Vessel represents for me a skilful monarch governing his vast States from his study and, while appearing immobile, causing everything to move.

But even if there is no Government that has more vigour, there is none in which the particular will has more empire and more easily dominates the rest. Everything moves towards the same end, to be sure; but this end is by no means that of public felicity, and the very strength of the Administration ceaselessly turns to the detriment of the State.

Kings wish to be absolute and are loudly informed that the best way of accomplishing this is to make their peoples love them. This maxim is very fine, and even very true in certain respects. Unfortunately Courts will always pay no heed to it. The power conferred by the love of peoples is no doubt the greatest; but, being precarious and conditional, it will never satisfy Princes. The best Kings wish to be able to be wicked if it pleases them, without ceasing to be masters. In vain will a political sermonizer tell them that, the people's strength being their strength, their highest interest is that the people should be flourishing, numerous and formidable: they know very well that this is not true. Their personal interest is primarily that the People should be weak, wretched and unable ever to resist them. I concede that, if you assume subjects who are always perfectly obedient, the interest of the Prince would then be that the people should be powerful, so that its power being his own would make him formidable to his neighbours. But as this interest is merely secondary and subordinate, and as the two assumptions are incompatible, it is natural that Princes always give preference to the maxim that is most directly useful to them. This is what Samuel pointed out forcefully to the Hebrews, and it is what Machiavelli clearly demonstrated. While professing to give lessons to Kings, he gave great lessons to their peoples. Machiavelli's *Prince* is the book of republicans.*

---

* Machiavelli was an honest man and a good citizen. But, being attached to the house of Medici, he was forced under the oppression of his fatherland to disguise his love of liberty. The very choice of his execrable Hero shows clearly enough his secret intention; and the contrast between the maxims

We found on the basis of general proportions that monarchy is suited only to large States, and we find the same thing if we examine it in itself. The more numerous the public administration is, the more the ratio between Prince and subjects diminishes and approaches parity, so that in Democracy this ratio is one, or parity itself. The same ratio increases in proportion to the contraction of the Government, and is at its *maximum* when the Government is in the hands of a single man. Then there is too great a distance between Prince and People, and the State lacks coherence. In order to achieve the latter, therefore, intermediary orders are necessary, and Princes, grandees and a nobility are needed to fill these. Now, nothing of all this is suited to a small State, which is ruined by all such degrees.

But if it is difficult for a large State to be well governed, it is far more so for it to be well governed by

---

of his book on the Prince and those in his discourses on Titus Livius and in his history of Florence shows that this profound political thinker has hitherto had only superficial or corrupt Readers. The Court of Rome severely proscribed his book, as I can well believe; for that court is what the book most clearly portrayed. [1782 edition]

a single man, and everyone knows what happens when the King gives himself deputies.

An essential and inevitable defect, which will always place monarchical below republican government, is the fact that in the latter the public vote almost never raises to the foremost positions any other than enlightened and capable men, who fill these with honour, whereas those who advance to them in monarchies are most often merely petty blunderers, petty rogues, petty schemers, who make use of the petty talents that in Courts bring advancement to great positions only to reveal their ineptitude to the public as soon as they have reached these. The people errs in its choice far less than the Prince, and a man of true merit is almost as rare in a ministry as a fool at the head of a republican government. So when, by some lucky chance, one of these men born to govern does take the helm of affairs in a Monarchy almost brought to ruin by such a fine pack of stewards, people are quite surprised by the resources he finds, and it represents a historic event for the country.

For a monarchical State to be well governed, its size or its extent would need to be tailored to the skills of the man who governs. It is easier to conquer than to rule. With a sufficient lever, you can shake the world with one finger; but to support it you need the shoulders of Hercules. If a State is large, the Prince is almost always too small. On the other hand, when it happens that the State is too small for its ruler, which is very rare, it is yet ill governed. For the ruler, still following the grandeur of his vision, forgets the interests of its peoples, and makes them no less wretched by the abuse of his excessive talents than does a limited ruler through the absence of the talents he lacks. A kingdom would, as it were, need to expand or contract with every reign, depending upon the Prince's capacity; whereas, with a Senate whose talents have more fixed quantities, the State can have stable boundaries and its administration run just as well.

The most evident disadvantage of Government by a single man is the lack of that continuous succession that in the other two forms provides an unbroken bond. One King dead, another is needed; elections allow dangerous intervals; they are stormy, and, unless the Citizens have a disinterestedness and integrity scarcely compatible with this type of Government,

intrigue and corruption come into play. It is hard for
a man to whom the State has been sold not to sell it
in turn, and not to seek compensation from the weak
for the money extorted from him by the powerful.
Sooner or later everything becomes venal under such
an administration, and then the peace enjoyed under
kings is worse than the disorder of interregna.

What has been done to forestall these ills? Crowns
have been made hereditary in certain families, and an
order of Succession has been established to forestall
any conflict upon the death of Kings. In other words,
replacing the disadvantage of elections by that of
regencies, a semblance of tranquillity has been preferred to a wise administration; and people have chosen
the risk of having a child, a monster or an idiot for a
ruler rather than to quarrel over the choice of a good
King. They have not considered that, by exposing
themselves thus to the risks of these alternatives, they
are pitting almost all the odds against them. There was
sound sense in what the young Dionysius would say
when his father, reproaching him for some shameful
action, asked: 'Did I set you such an example?' 'No,'
the son replied, 'but your father was not a king.'

Everything conspires to deprive a man brought up

to command others of justice and reason. It is said that great trouble is taken to teach young Princes the art of ruling; this education does not appear to benefit them. People would do better to begin by teaching them the art of obedience. The greatest kings celebrated by history have not been brought up to rule at all. It is a knowledge that is never possessed less than when it has been too much learned, and that is better acquired by obeying than by commanding. *Nam utilissimus idem ac brevissimus bonarum malarumque rerum delectus, cogitare quid aut nolueris sub alio Principe aut volueris* [For the best and shortest way of choosing between good things and bad is to consider what you will have either wished for or not wished for under another Prince].*

One result of this lack of coherence is the inconstancy of royal government, which follows sometimes one plan and sometimes another, depending on the character of the Prince who rules or of the people who rule for him, so cannot for long have any fixed object or consistent conduct: a variability that always causes the State to drift from maxim to maxim, from project to project, and that does not occur in other

* Tacitus, *Histories*, Book I.

Governments in which the Prince is always the same. It can also be seen that in general, if there is more guile in a Court, there is more wisdom in a Senate; and that Republics pursue their aims with more constant and coherent views, whereas every revolution in a Ministry produces one in the State – since the maxim common to all Ministries, and almost all Kings, is to do the reverse in all things of what their predecessor did.

This same incoherence gives the lie to a sophism very common among royalist political thinkers, which is not merely to compare civil Government to domestic Government and the prince to the paterfamilias, an error refuted earlier, but also to bestow liberally upon that magistrate all the virtues he would need, and always to assume that the Prince is what he ought to be: an assumption thanks to which royal Government is evidently preferable to any other, because it is undeniably the strongest, and because in order to be also the best it lacks only a corporate will more in conformity with the general will.

But if, according to Plato,* the King by nature is

---

*   In *The Statesman*.

so rare a personage, how often will nature and fortune combine to crown him; and if the kingly education necessarily corrupts those who receive it, what is to be hoped of a succession of men brought up to rule? So it would be a great mistake to confuse royal Government with government by a good King. In order to see what this Government is in itself, it must be considered under limited or wicked Princes; for they will arrive such on the Throne, or the Throne will make them such.

These difficulties have not escaped our Authors, but they are by no means troubled by them. The remedy, they say, is to obey without grumbling. God in his wrath sends bad Kings, and they must be borne as punishments from Heaven. This argument is doubtless edifying; but I wonder if it might not be more fitting in the pulpit than in a political work. What would we say of a Doctor who promised miracles, and all of whose skill consisted in exhorting his invalid to be patient? Everyone knows that you must suffer a bad Government when you have one; the question is how to find a good one.

CHAPTER 7
Of Mixed Governments

Properly speaking, there is no simple Government. A single ruler must have subordinate magistrates; a popular Government must have a head. Hence, in the division of executive power, there is always a gradation from the large number to the lesser, with this difference that sometimes the large number depends upon the small, and sometimes the small upon the large.

At times there is an equal division. Either when the constituent parts are in mutual dependence, as in the Government of England; or when the authority of each part is independent but imperfect, as in Poland. This latter form is bad, because there is no unity in the Government, and the State lacks cohesion.

Which is better, a simple Government or a mixed Government? This is a question hotly debated among political thinkers, and to which the same answer must be given that I gave earlier regarding any form of Government.

A simple Government is best in itself, just because it is simple. But when the executive Power does not sufficiently depend upon the legislature, viz. when there is more of a relation between Prince and Sovereign than between People and Prince, it is necessary to remedy this lack of proportion by dividing the Government; for then all its parts have no less authority over the subjects, while their division makes them all together less strong against the Sovereign.

The same disadvantage is guarded against also by establishing intermediate magistrates, who, while leaving the Government in its entirety, serve only to balance the two Powers and to maintain their respective rights. Then Government is not mixed, but tempered.

The opposite disadvantage may be remedied by similar means, erecting Tribunals to reinforce Government when it is too weak. That is practised in all Democracies. In the former case, Government is divided in order to weaken it, and in the latter in order to strengthen it. For the *maximum* degrees of strength and weakness are alike to be found in simple Governments, whereas mixed forms of the latter give an average strength.

CHAPTER 8

*How Every Form of Government
Does Not Suit Every Country*

Liberty, not being a fruit of every Clime, is not within the reach of all peoples. The more you reflect upon this principle established by Montesquieu, the more you sense its truth. The more you deny it, the more opportunity you provide to establish it by new evidence.

In all the world's Governments, the public person consumes but produces nothing. So whence comes the substance consumed? From the labour of its members. It is the surplus of individuals that produces the wherewithal of the public. Whence it follows that the civil state can subsist only so long as the labour of men yields more than their needs.

Now this excess is not the same in all countries of the world. In several it is considerable, in others mediocre, in others nil, in others negative. This proportion depends upon the fertility of the climate, upon the kind of labour that the land demands, upon the nature of its production, upon the strength of its inhabitants, upon the greater or lesser consumption that is necessary to them, and upon several other similar proportions that make it up.

On the other hand, all Governments are not of the same kind. Some devour more, some less, and the differences are based on this other principle, that the more distant the public contributions are from their source, the more onerous they are. It is not in terms of the quantity of levies that this burden is to be measured, but in terms of the path these have to follow in order to return to the hands whence they emerged. When this circulation is speedy and well established, whether little is paid or much does not matter; the people is still rich and the finances are still healthy. On the other hand, however little the People may give, when this little does not come back to it at all, by continuing to give it is soon exhausted; the State is never rich, and the people is still wretched.

It follows from this that the more the distance between people and Government increases, the more onerous the tribute becomes. Hence, in Democracy the people is least burdened, in Aristocracy it is more so, in Monarchy it carries the heaviest load. So Monarchy suits only opulent nations, Aristocracy suits

States of middling wealth and size, Democracy suits small and poor States.

Indeed, the more you reflect, the more difference between free and monarchical States you find in the following: while in the former everything is used for the common utility; in the latter the public force and individual forces are reciprocal, the former increasing through weakening of the latter. In short, instead of governing subjects in order to make them happy, despotism makes them wretched in order to govern them.

Clearly, therefore, in every climate there are natural causes which make it possible to assign the form of Government necessitated by the climate, and even to say what kind of inhabitants it must have. Thankless, sterile places where the produce does not repay the labour must remain uncultivated and deserted, or peopled only by Savages. Places where human labour yields only bare necessities must be inhabited by barbarous peoples; any polity would be impossible there. Places where the surplus of produce over labour is middling suit free peoples. Those where abundant, fertile land gives much produce for little labour need to be governed monarchically, so that the surplus of the excess subjects may be consumed through the luxury of the Prince. For it is better that this surplus be absorbed by the government than dissipated by individuals. There are exceptions, I know; but these very exceptions confirm the rule, in that they sooner or later produce revolutions that bring things back to the order of nature.

We must always distinguish general laws from the particular causes that can modify their effect. If the entire south were covered by Republics and the entire north by despotic States, it would be no less true that in terms of climate despotism suits hot countries, barbarism cold countries, and a good polity suits intermediate regions. I see too that while granting the principle, you could still argue over the application; you could say that there are very fertile cold countries and very barren southern ones. But this difficulty is one only for those who do not examine the matter in all its aspects. As I have already said, account must be taken of such factors as labour, strength, consumption, etc.

Let us assume two equal tracts, one yielding five units and the other ten. If the inhabitants of the former consume four and those of the latter nine, the surplus product of the former will be one-fifth and that of the latter one-tenth. The ratio between these two surpluses thus being the inverse of that between the two yields, the tract producing only five will give double the surplus of the tract producing ten.

But there is no question of the produce being double, and I do not think that anybody would dare in general to place the fertility of cold countries on an equal footing with that of hot ones. Let us, however, assume such equality. Let us allow, if you wish, England to balance out Sicily, Poland Egypt. Further to the south we shall have Africa and the Indies, further to the north we shall no longer have anything. For this equality of produce, what difference in cultivation? In Sicily it is necessary only to scratch the earth, in England what hard work to till it! Now, wherever more manpower is needed to yield the same product, the surplus must necessarily be less.

Apart from that, consider that the same quantity of men consumes much less in hot countries. The climate requires that people be abstemious there in order to be healthy: Europeans who wish to live there as at home all perish of dysentery or indigestion.

'We are carnivorous beasts,' says Chardin, 'wolves, in comparison with Asiatics. Some people attribute the abstemiousness of the Persians to the fact that their country is less cultivated, but for my part I think that their country is less abundant in foodstuffs because its inhabitants require less. If their frugality', he continues, 'was an effect of the country's dearth, only the poor would eat little, whereas it is generally everyone; and people would eat more or less in every province according to the fertility of the land, whereas the same abstemiousness is found throughout the kingdom. They are very boastful about their way of living, saying that it is necessary only to look at their complexion in order to recognize how much more excellent this way of living is than that of Christians. Indeed the complexion of the Persians is smooth, they have a beautiful, fine, polished skin; whereas the complexion of the Armenians, their subjects who live in the European manner, is coarse and blotchy, and their bodies are big and heavy.'

The closer you come to the equator, the more peoples live off little. They scarcely eat meat: rice, maize, couscous, millet and cassava are their usual victuals. In the Indies there are millions of men whose food costs less than a *sou* a day. In Europe itself we see perceptible differences in appetite between the peoples of the north and those of the south. A Spaniard will live for eight days off a German's dinner. In the countries where men are greediest, luxury thus turns towards articles of consumption. In England, it is visible on a table laden with meats; in Italy you are regaled with sugar and flowers.

Luxury of apparel too presents similar differences. In climates where seasonal changes are speedy and violent, you have better and simpler costumes; in those where people dress only for finery, a striking effect is prized over usefulness and the costumes themselves are a luxury. In Naples you will every day see men in gold-braided coats but no stockings walking on Mount Pausillipus. It is the same thing for buildings: magnificence is the prime concern when there is nothing to fear from draughts. In Paris or London people wish to be lodged warmly and comfortably. In Madrid people have splendid drawing-rooms, but no windows that close, and sleep in garrets.

Foods are far more substantial and succulent in hot countries. This is a third difference that cannot fail to influence the second. Why do people eat so many vegetables in Italy? Because these are good

79

and nourishing there, and taste excellent. In France where they are fed only with water, they give no nourishment; and count for almost nothing on people's tables. Yet they occupy no less farmland, and take at least as much trouble to cultivate. It has been shown by experiment that the wheats of Barbary, albeit inferior to those of France, yield far more flour, and that those of France in turn yield more than the wheats of the North. Whence it may be inferred that a similar gradation is observed generally in the same direction from the equator to the pole. Now, is it not an evident disadvantage to have in an equal produce a lesser quantity of food?

To all these different considerations I can add one that derives from them and that reinforces them: it is the fact that hot countries have less need of inhabitants than cold countries, and could feed more of them, which produces a double surplus still favouring despotism. The larger the area that a certain number of inhabitants occupies, the more difficult rebellion becomes; for it is not possible to confer speedily and in secret, and it is always easy for the Government to get wind of projects and cut communications. But the more tightly a numerous people is crowded together, the less the Government can encroach upon the Sovereign; the latter's rulers deliberate as securely in their rooms as the Prince in his council-chamber, and the mob assembles as soon in the market-places as the troops in their barracks. The advantage of a tyrannical Government thus consists in its ability to act over long distances. With the aid of the fulcra it provides for itself, its strength increases from afar like that of a lever.* The strength of the people, on the other hand, acts only when concentrated; it evaporates and is lost when it spreads, like the effect of gun-powder scattered on the ground which ignites only grain by grain. The least populated countries are thus most suitable for Tyranny: savage beasts reign only in wildernesses.

* This does not contradict what I said earlier in Book II, chapter 9, on the disadvantages of large States. For there it was a matter of the Government's authority over its members, while here it is a matter of its strength against its subjects. Its scattered members serve it as fulcra to act upon the people from afar, but it has no fulcrum to act directly upon those members themselves. Thus in one case the length of the lever makes for weakness, in the other for strength.

CHAPTER 9
Of the Signs of a Good Government

So when you ask in absolute terms what the best Government is, you pose a question at once insoluble and indeterminate. Or, if you like, it has as many good solutions as there are possible combinations in the absolute and relative positions of peoples.

But if you asked by what sign you can tell whether a given people is well governed or ill, that would be another thing, and the question might in fact be resolved.

However, it is not resolved at all, because everyone wishes to resolve it in their own way. Subjects extol public tranquillity, Citizens the liberty of individuals; one man prefers security of ownership, another personal security; one man deems the strictest Government best, another maintains that it is the mildest; this man wants crimes to be punished, that one wishes them to be prevented; one likes the idea of being feared by neighbours, another prefers to be ignored by them; one is content when money circulates, another demands that the people should have bread. Even if people could agree on these points and others like them, would they be any further forward? Since moral quantities lack a precise measure, if people were agreed on the sign, how would they agree on the assessment?

For my part, I am always astonished that so simple a sign should go unrecognized, and that people should have the bad faith not to acknowledge it. What is the purpose of political association? It is the preservation and prosperity of its members. And what is the surest sign that these are preserved and prospering? It is their numbers and [increasing] population. So do not look elsewhere for this much disputed sign. All other things being equal, the Government under which Citizens – without such external means as naturalization or colonies – increase and multiply most is infallibly the best. The one under which a people dwindles and declines is the worst. Reckoners, it is now up to you: count, measure, compare.*

---

* We should follow the same principle in judging which centuries merit our preference in terms of the prosperity of mankind. We have admired too much those in which letters and arts have been seen to flourish, without grasping the secret aim of their cultivation, and without considering its fateful effect, *idque apud imperitos humanitas vocabatur, cum*

CHAPTER 10

Of the Abuse of Government and
Its Tendency to Degenerate

As the individual will constantly acts against the general will, so does the Government make a continual effort against Sovereignty. The more this effort increases, the more the constitution deteriorates; and since there is no other corporate will here that, by

---

pars servitutis esset [and the ignorant called it 'human nature', whereas it was part of slavery]. In the maxims of books, shall we never see the vulgar interest that makes their Authors speak? No, whatever they may say about it, when a country becomes depopulated in spite of its brilliance, it is not true that all is going well; and it is not enough for a poet to have an income of a hundred thousand *livres* for his century to be best of all. We should pay less regard to the apparent ease and tranquillity of rulers than to the well-being of whole nations, and above all of the most populous states. Hail may lay waste a few cantons, but it rarely brings a famine. Riots and civil wars greatly frighten rulers, but they do not cause the true misfortunes of peoples, which can even have some respite while argument rages over who will tyrannize them. It is their permanent state which gives birth to their real prosperity or their real calamities. It is when everything remains crushed beneath the yoke that everything declines,

resisting, can balance that of the Prince, it must happen sooner or later that the Prince will at last oppress the Sovereign and break the Social treaty. This is the inherent and inevitable vice that from the birth of the body politic tends unremittingly to destroy it, just as old age and death destroy the body of man.

There are two general ways whereby a Government degenerates: viz. when it contracts, or when the State is dissolved.

---

and that rulers, destroying them with ease, *ubi solitudinem faciunt, pacem appellant* [where they create solitude, call it peace]. When the bickerings of the Nobles were disrupting the kingdom of France, and the Coadjutor of Paris used to go to Parliament with a dagger in his pocket, that did not prevent the French people, happy and numerous, from living at their ease in respectability and liberty. In olden times Greece flourished amid the cruellest wars; blood flowed copiously, yet the whole land was filled with men. It seemed, Machiavelli says, that amid murders, banishments and civil wars our [Florentine] Republic grew all the more powerful; the virtue of its citizens, their morals and their independence had more effect in strengthening it than all its disputes had in weakening it. A little unrest gives vigour to the soul, and what makes the species truly prosper is not so much peace as liberty.

The Government contracts when it passes from the many to the few: in other words, from Democracy to Aristocracy, and from Aristocracy to Monarchy. That is its natural tendency.* If it regressed from the few

---

* The slow formation and the progress of the Republic of Venice in its lagoons offers a notable example of this succession. And it is astonishing indeed that after more than twelve hundred years the Venetians seem still to be only at the second stage, which began at the *Serrar del Consiglio* in 1198. As for the old Doges who are brought up against them, whatever the *Squitinio della libertà veneta* may say about them, it is proven that they were not their Sovereigns at all. People will not fail to cite against me the Roman Republic, which they will claim followed a quite opposite progress, passing from monarchy to Aristocracy, and from Aristocracy to Democracy. I am very far from viewing things like this.

The first establishment of Romulus was a mixed Government, which quickly degenerated into Despotism. For specific reasons the State perished before its time, as a newborn child sometimes dies before having reached manhood. The expulsion of the Tarquins was the true epoch when the Republic was born. But it did not at first take a constant form, because by not abolishing the patriciate only half the work was done. For in this way the hereditary Aristocracy, which is the worst of legitimate administrations, remained in conflict with Democracy, so that the still uncertain and fluctuating form of Government was settled, as Machiavelli proved, only when the Tribunes were established; then alone was there a true Government and a true Democracy. In fact the people was

to the many, it could be said to loosen, but this inverse movement is impossible.

Indeed, the Government never changes form except when its worn mainspring leaves it too much enfeebled to retain its original form. Now, if through expansion it were to slacken still further, its strength would become entirely null, and even less would it survive. So it is necessary to rewind and tighten the

---

then not merely Sovereign, but also magistrate and judge, the Senate was merely a subsidiary tribunal to moderate or concentrate the Government, and the Consuls themselves, albeit Patricians, albeit first Magistrates, albeit absolute Generals in war, in Rome were only the presidents of the people.

Thenceforth the Government too was seen to take its natural tendency and to incline strongly to Aristocracy. With the Patriciate being abolished almost of its own accord, Aristocracy was no longer in the body of Patricians as it is in Venice and Genoa, but in the body of the Senate made up of Patricians and Plebeians, even in the body of the Tribunes when these began to usurp an active power; for words do nothing to things, and when the people has rulers who govern for it, whatever name these rulers bear, it is always an Aristocracy. From the abuse of Aristocracy sprang the civil wars and the Triumvirate. Sulla, Julius Caesar, Augustus became in fact real Monarchs, and finally under the Despotism of Tiberius the State was dissolved. Roman history thus does not refute my principle, it confirms it.

mainspring even as it yields, otherwise the State it sustains would founder.

Dissolution of the State can come about in two ways.

The first is when the Prince no longer administers the State in keeping with the laws, but usurps the sovereign power. Then a remarkable change takes place. For it is not the Government but the State that contracts. I mean that the great State is dissolved, and another is formed within it, composed only of the members of the Government, which to the rest of the People is no longer anything but its master and tyrant, in such a way that, at the instant when the Government usurps sovereignty, the social pact is broken; and all simple Citizens, restored by right to their natural liberty, are forced – albeit not obliged – to obey.

The same thing also comes about when the members of the Government usurp severally the power that they should exercise only as a body; which is no less an infraction of the laws, and produces still greater disorder. Then you have, so to speak, as many Princes as Magistrates, and the State, no less divided than the Government, perishes or changes form.

When the State dissolves, abuse of the Government, whatever it may be, takes the common name of *anarchy*. To distinguish further, Democracy degenerates into *Ochlocracy*, Aristocracy into *Oligarchy*; I would add that Monarchy degenerates into *Tyranny*, but this latter word is ambiguous and requires some explanation.

In the vulgar sense, a Tyrant is a King who governs with violence and without regard to justice and the laws. In the precise sense, a Tyrant is an individual who arrogates to himself royal authority without having any right to it. It is thus that the Greeks understood this word Tyrant. They gave it indifferently to good and bad Princes whose authority was not legitimate.* Thus *Tyrant* and *Usurper* are two entirely synonymous words.

---

* *Omnes enim et habentur et dicuntur Tyranni qui potestate utuntur perpetua, in ea Civitate quae libertate usa est* [For all are both deemed and called Tyrants who use perpetual power, in that City which is used to liberty], Cornelius Nepos, *Life of Miltiades*. It is true that Aristotle in *Nichomachean Ethics*, Book VIII, chapter X, distinguishes the Tyrant from the King, in that the former governs for his own utility and the latter only for the utility of his subjects. But apart from the fact that all Greek authors generally took the word Tyrant in another sense, as

To give different names to different things, I call *Tyrant* the usurper of royal authority, and *Despot* the usurper of Sovereign power. The Tyrant is he who interferes against the laws in order to govern according to the laws; the Despot is he who places himself above the laws themselves. Thus the Tyrant can be no Despot, but the Despot is always a Tyrant.

CHAPTER 11
Of the Death of the Body Politic

Such is the natural and inevitable trend of the best constituted Governments. If Sparta and Rome perished, what State can hope to last for ever? Hence, if we wish to form a lasting institution, let us not think about making it eternal. In order to succeed we should not attempt the impossible, or flatter ourselves that we are giving the work of men a solidity that does not belong to human things.

---

appears above all from the *Hieron* of Xenophon, it would follow from Aristotle's distinction that since the beginning of the world there would never have existed a single King.

The body politic, as much as the human body, begins to die from its birth on, and bears within itself the causes of its destruction. But both may have a constitution that is more robust or less, fit to preserve it for a longer or shorter time. The constitution of man is the work of nature, that of the State is the work of artifice. It does not depend upon men to prolong their life, it does depend upon them as far as possible to prolong that of the State, by giving it the best constitution it could have. The best constituted one will come to an end, but later than others, if no unforeseen accident brings it to destruction before its time.

The principle of political life is in Sovereign authority. Legislative power is the heart of the State, executive power is its brain, which gives movement to every part. The brain may become paralysed, yet the individual still lives. A man is left an imbecile and lives. But as soon as the heart has ceased its functions, the animal is dead.

It is by no means through laws that the State subsists, it is through legislative power. Yesterday's law does not bind today, but tacit consent is presumed from silence, and the Sovereign is deemed ceaselessly to confirm laws that he does not abrogate, though he could do so. All that he ever proclaimed as his will, he still wills, unless he revokes it.

So why do people accord such respect to old laws? It is for that very reason. They must believe that it is only the excellence of former wills that could have preserved them for so long; if the Sovereign had not continuously acknowledged them as beneficial, he would have revoked them a thousand times. That is why, far from growing weaker, laws constantly acquire new force in every well-constituted State; the bias in favour of antiquity makes them daily more venerable. On the other hand, wherever laws grow weaker as they age, this proves that there is no longer any legislative power, and that the State is no longer alive.

CHAPTER 12
How Sovereign Authority Is Maintained

The Sovereign, having no force other than legislative power, acts only through laws; and laws being merely authentic acts of the general will, the Sovereign should be capable of acting only when the people is assembled. The people assembled, you will say! What a pipe-dream! It is a pipe-dream today, but two thousand years ago it was not. Have men changed their nature?

The limits of the possible in moral things are less narrow than we think. It is our weaknesses, our vices and our prejudices that shrink them. Mean spirits do not believe in great men at all; vile slaves smile mockingly at the word liberty.

Let what has been done show us what can be done. I shall not speak of the ancient republics of Greece, but the Roman republic seems to me to have been a great State, and the city of Rome a great city. The last census recorded four hundred thousand Citizens bearing arms in Rome, and the last count of the Empire more than four million Citizens without including subjects, foreigners, women, children or slaves.

How hard might you imagine it to be, frequently to assemble the vast people of that capital and its surroundings? Yet few weeks went by without the Roman people being assembled, even several times. It exercised not merely the rights of sovereignty, but in part those of Government. It used to deal with certain affairs, judge certain cases, and on the market-place that whole people was magistrate almost as often as Citizen.

If you went back to the earliest days of Nations, you would find that most ancient governments, even monarchical ones like those of the Macedonians and the Franks, had similar Councils. Be that as it may, this one incontestable fact answers all difficulties. Arguing from what has existed to what is possible seems valid to me.

CHAPTER 13

*How Sovereign Authority Is Maintained –
continued*

It is not enough that the assembled people should once have fixed the constitution of the State by giving its sanction to a body of laws; it is not enough that it should have established a perpetual Government or that it should have provided once and for all for the election of magistrates. Apart from the extraordinary assemblies that unforeseen cases can demand, it is necessary that there should be fixed and periodic ones that nothing can abolish or adjourn, so that on the appointed day the people is legitimately summoned together by law, without this requiring any other formal summons.

But outside of these assemblies that are juridical by virtue of their date alone, every assembly of the People that has not been summoned by the magistrates appointed for that purpose and according to the prescribed forms must be deemed illegitimate and everything done at it deemed null; because the very order to assemble must emanate from the law.

As for the more or less frequent recurrence of legitimate assemblies, this depends upon so many considerations that precise rules could not be given in that respect. You can merely say in general that the more strength the Government has, the more frequently the Sovereign must appear.

This may be fine for a single town, you will say, but what is to be done when the State contains several? Is Sovereign authority to be shared, or should you concentrate it in a single town and subjugate all the rest?

I reply that neither one thing nor the other should be done. First of all, sovereign authority is simple and single, and it cannot be divided without destroying it. In the second place, a town cannot legitimately be subjugated to another any more than can a Nation, because the essence of the body politic lies in the reconciliation of obedience and liberty, and because these words *subject* and *sovereign* are identical correlatives whose meaning is united in the single word Citizen.

I reply further that it is always wrong to unite several towns in a single city, and that if you do seek to make such a union you should not flatter yourself that you can avoid its natural disadvantages. Abuse by great States should not be put forward as a counter-argument against someone who desires only small ones. But how may small States be given enough strength to resist great ones? As the Greek towns formerly resisted the great King, and as more recently Holland and Switzerland have resisted the house of Austria.

However, if the State cannot be reduced to proper limits, one recourse still remains; this is not to permit a capital at all, to have the Government sit in each town successively, and likewise to convene all the country's Estates in each by turn.

Populate the territory evenly, extend the same rights throughout it, carry abundance and life throughout it: that is how the State will become at once the strongest and the best governed possible. Remember that town walls are formed only from the wreckage of cottages. Whenever I see a Palace raised in the capital, I have visions of a whole countryside cast into hovels.

CHAPTER 14
How Sovereign Authority Is Maintained – continued

The moment the People is legitimately assembled as a Sovereign body, all the Government's jurisdiction ceases, executive power is suspended, and the person of the humblest Citizen is as sacred and inviolable as that of the highest Magistrate, because where the Represented is present there is no longer any Representative. Most conflicts that broke out in the comitia of Rome came from ignorance or neglect of this rule.

The Consuls were then only Presidents of the People, the Tribunes mere Speakers,* the Senate was nothing at all.

These intervals of suspension, when the Prince recognizes – or should recognize – a present superior, have always been threatening to it; and these assemblies of the people, which are the aegis of the body politic and a curb on Government, have always filled rulers with dread. Hence, they regularly spare no endeavours, objections, obstructions or promises in order to discourage Citizens from them. When the latter are greedy, cowardly and pusillanimous, loving ease more than liberty, they do not long hold out against the redoubled efforts of the Government. In this way, as the force of resistance constantly increases, the Sovereign authority eventually evaporates, so that most cities fall and perish before their time.

But between Sovereign authority and arbitrary Government there is sometimes interposed an

---

* More or less in the sense given to this term in the Parliament of England. The similarity between these functions would have brought the Consuls and the Tribunes into conflict even if all jurisdiction had been suspended.

intermediate power, about which something must be said.

CHAPTER 15
Of Deputies or Representatives

As soon as public service ceases to be the main business of Citizens, and they prefer to serve with their purses than with their persons, the State is already near to its ruin. Is it necessary to go into combat? They pay troops and stay at home. Is it necessary to enter the Council? They nominate Deputies and stay at home. Helped by indolence and money, they end up with soldiers to serve the fatherland and representatives to sell it.

It is the hurly-burly of commerce and the arts, it is avid pursuit of gain, it is softness and love of comfort, that commute personal services into money. You yield part of your profit in order to increase it at your leisure. Give money, and soon you will have shackles. This word *finance* is a slave's word: it is unknown in the City. In a truly free State, citizens do everything with their own hands and nothing with money. Far from paying to be exempted from their duties, they would pay to fulfil these themselves. I am very far from the common opinion: I consider labour dues less contrary to liberty than taxes.

The better the State is constituted, the more do public affairs prevail over private in the minds of its Citizens. There is even far less in the way of private affairs, since with the sum of common happiness providing a more considerable portion of each individual's own, less remains for him to seek in personal concerns. In a well-conducted city everyone flies to assemblies; under a bad Government no one cares to take a step to reach them. For no one takes any interest in what is done there, the general will is not expected to prevail there, and lastly domestic concerns are all-absorbing. Good laws cause better ones to be made, bad laws bring worse. As soon as anyone says of State affairs: *what do I care?*, you must reckon that the State is lost.

Cooling of love for the fatherland, the activity of private interest, the immensity of States, conquests, and abuse of Government – all these have led people to devise the procedure of Deputies or Representatives of the people in the Nation's assemblies. This is what in certain countries they dare to call the Third

Estate, which means that the particular interest of two orders is ranked first and second, while the public interest is only third.

Sovereignty cannot be represented, for the same reason that it cannot be alienated. It consists essentially in the general will, and will cannot be represented: it is the same or it is other – there is no middle ground. Hence, the deputies of the people are not and cannot be its representatives; they are merely its agents, who cannot conclude anything definitively. Any law that the People has not ratified in person is null; it is no law at all. The English people thinks it is free, but it is quite mistaken: it is free only during the election of members of Parliament; as soon as these are elected, it is enslaved, it is nothing. The use it makes of its brief moments of liberty fully warrants its loss of it.

The idea of Representatives is modern. It comes to us from feudal Government, from that iniquitous and absurd Government which degrades the human race and dishonours the name of man. In ancient Republics and even monarchies, the People never had representatives: that word was not known. It is very striking that in Rome, where the Tribunes were so sacred, no one ever imagined that they might usurp the functions of the people; striking that in the midst of so great a multitude they never attempted to pass a single Plebiscite on their own authority. Yet the trouble the mob sometimes caused may be judged by what happened at the time of the Gracchi, when a portion of the Citizens cast their votes from the rooftops.

Where rights and liberty are everything, inconveniences are nothing. Among that wise people, everything was given its just due: it used to allow its Lictors to do what its Tribunes would never have dared to do; it had no fear that its Lictors might seek to represent it.

However, in order to explain how the Tribunes sometimes used to represent the People, it is enough to grasp how the Government represents the Sovereign. Since the Law is but a declaration of the general will, it is clear that in its Legislative power the People cannot be represented. But it can and must be represented in its executive power, which is simply force applied to the Law. This makes clear that, if things were examined properly, it would be found that very few Nations have laws. Be that as it may, the Tribunes, having no portion of the executive power, could certainly never represent the Roman People by virtue of the rights their posts conferred, but only by usurp-ing the rights of the Senate.

Among the Greeks, the People used to do for itself all that it had to do; it continually assembled on the market-place. It lived in a mild climate; it was not at all greedy; slaves did its work; its chief concern was its liberty. No longer having the same advantages, how are you to preserve the same rights? Your harsher climes add to your needs,* for six months in the year the market-place is uninhabitable, your flat tongues cannot make themselves heard in the open, you care more for your profit than for your liberty, and you fear slavery far less than destitution.

What! Is liberty to be maintained only with the support of servitude? Perhaps. The two extremes meet. Everything unknown to nature has its disadvantages, and civil society more than all the rest. There are cer-tain unfortunate situations in which you can preserve your liberty only at the expense of that of others, and in which the Citizen cannot be entirely free without

---

* To adopt in cold countries the luxury and softness of Orien-tals is to be willing to accept their chains, indeed to submit to these even more inevitably than they do.

the slave being utterly enslaved. Such was the situation in Sparta. For you, modern peoples, you have no slaves, but you are slaves; you pay for their liberty with your own. In vain do you boast of this preference: I find more cowardice in it than humanity.

I certainly do not mean by all this that it is necessary to have slaves, nor that the right to enslave is legitimate, since I have proved the opposite. I am merely stating the reasons why modern peoples which think themselves free have Representatives, and why ancient peoples had none. Be that as it may, from the moment that a People gives itself Representatives, it ceases to be free; it ceases to be.

Having examined everything carefully, I do not see how it is henceforth possible for the Sovereign to preserve among us the exercise of its rights, if the City be not very small. But if it is very small, surely it will be subjugated? No. How the external power of a great People can be combined with the easy administration and good order of a small State I shall demonstrate hereafter.*

---

*   This is what I had proposed to do in the remainder of this work, when, in dealing with external relations, I came to

CHAPTER 16
How the Institution of Government Is No Contract

Once the Legislative power is well established, the executive power must be established in similar fashion. For the latter, which operates only through particular acts, being essentially different from the former is necessarily separate from it. If it was possible for the Sovereign, considered as such, to have the executive power, right and fact would be so confused that you would no longer know what was law and what was not, and the body politic, thus disfigured, would be prey to the violence against which it was instituted.

Since the Citizens are all equal through the social contract, all may prescribe what all must do, whereas no one has the right to require another to do what he does not do himself. Yet it is this very right, indispensable for giving the body politic life and motion, that the Sovereign confers on the Prince by instituting Government.

_____

confederations. This is a wholly new topic, and one whose principles remain to be established.

Some have maintained that this act of establishing a Government was a contract between the People and its chosen rulers: a contract stipulating between the two parties the conditions under which one undertook to command and the other to obey. You will agree, I am sure, that this is a strange way to make a contract! But let us see if this opinion is tenable.

In the first place, the supreme authority can no more be modified than it can be alienated; to limit it is to destroy it. It is absurd and contradictory for the Sovereign to give itself a superior; to bind itself to obey a master is to return to absolute liberty.

Furthermore, it is evident that this contract between the people and specific persons would be a particular act. Whence it follows that this contract could not be a law or an act of sovereignty, and that consequently it would be illegitimate.

It is also clear that the contracting parties would between themselves be subject to the law of nature alone, and without any guarantee of their reciprocal undertakings, which is wholly repugnant to the civil state. Since whoever has force at his command is always the master of what is done, you might equally well apply the word 'contract' to the act of a man who says to another: 'I shall give you all my goods, on condition that you give me back whatever you please.'

There is only one contract in the State, which is the contract of association; of itself alone it excludes all others. No public Contract could be imagined that was not a violation of this first.

CHAPTER 17
Of the Institution of Government

In what terms should we conceive of the act whereby Government is instituted? I shall begin by remarking that this act is complex, or composed of two others: viz. the establishment of law, and the execution of law.

By the former, the Sovereign decrees that a body of Government will be established in such and such a form; and it is clear that this act is a law.

By the latter, the People names the rulers who will be entrusted with the established Government. Now this nomination, being a particular act, is not a second law; it is merely a continuation of the first and a function of Government.

The difficulty is to understand how there can be

an act of Government before Government exists, and how the People, which is only either Sovereign or subject, can in certain circumstances become a Prince or Magistrate.

Here again is revealed one of those astonishing properties of the body politic, whereby it reconciles apparently contradictory operations. For this is accomplished by a sudden conversion of Sovereignty into Democracy, in such a way that, without any perceptible change, and simply through a new relation of all to all, the Citizens, having become Magistrates, pass from general acts to particular acts, and from law to execution.

This changed relation is by no means a speculative ploy without any example in practice. It takes place daily in the Parliament of England, where the lower House on certain occasions turns into a Grand Committee, the better to discuss its business, and thus becomes a mere commission of the Sovereign Court that it was a moment before, in such a way that it later reports to itself as the House of Commons on what it has just settled in Grand Committee, and deliberates anew in one capacity on what it has already decided in another.

It is the peculiar advantage of Democratic Government that it can be established in fact by a simple act of the general will. After this, either this provisional Government remains in office, if such is the form adopted; or in the Sovereign's name it establishes the Government prescribed by law, and all is thus in order. It is not possible to institute Government in any other legitimate way, and without renouncing the principles established earlier.

CHAPTER 18
Means of Preventing Usurpations by Government

In confirmation of Chapter 17, these clarifications show that the act instituting Government is no contract but a Law; that those in whom the executive power is vested are not the people's masters, but its officers; that the people can appoint them and dismiss them as it pleases; that it is a matter for them not of contracting, but of obeying; and that in assuming the functions which the State imposes on them, they are merely fulfilling their duty as Citizens, without having any sort of right to argue over the conditions.

So when the People happens to institute a hereditary Government, either monarchical in one family
or aristocratic in one order of Citizens, it is making
no kind of commitment, but giving a provisional
form to the administration, until it is pleased to order
things otherwise.

It is true that such changes are always dangerous,
and that the established Government should never
be touched except when it becomes incompatible
with the public weal; but this circumspection is a
maxim of politics not a rule of right, and the State
is no more bound to leave civil authority to its rulers
than military authority to its Generals.

It is true too that in such cases the greatest care
must be taken to observe all the formalities required
in order to distinguish a regular and legitimate act
from a seditious tumult, and the will of an entire
people from the clamour of a faction. It is here, above
all, that invidious cases must be dealt with only by
what strict application of the law demands. It is from
this same obligation that the Prince derives a great
advantage for preserving its power in defiance of
the people, without anyone being able to say that it
has usurped that power. For while seeming only to

exercise its rights, it can very easily extend these and on the pretext of public calm prevent assemblies intended to re-establish good order. So it exploits a silence that it prevents from being broken, or irregularities for which it is responsible, to claim it is favoured by the assent of those silenced by fear and to punish those who dare to speak. Thus did the Decemvirs, having first been elected for a year then kept on for another year, attempt to keep their power in perpetuity, by no longer allowing the comitia to assemble. And it is by this simple means that all the governments of the world, once invested with public force, sooner or later usurp the Sovereign authority.

The periodic assemblies of which I spoke above are suitable for forestalling or postponing this evil, above all when they require no formal convocation. For then the Prince could not prevent them without declaring itself openly a lawbreaker and enemy of the State.

These assemblies, whose sole purpose is maintenance of the social treaty, should always open with two motions that can never be omitted, to be voted on separately.

The first: *if it please the Sovereign to maintain the present form of Government.*

The second: *if it please the People to leave the administration to those at present charged with it.*

I assume here what I believe I have demonstrated, viz. that in the State there is no fundamental law that cannot be revoked, not even the social pact. For if all the Citizens came together to break this pact by common accord, one cannot doubt but that it would be very legitimately broken. Grotius even thinks that anyone can renounce the State of which he is a member, and recover his natural liberty and his goods by leaving the country.* Now, it would be absurd if the Citizens united could not do what each of them can do separately.

End of the Third Book

---

*   Provided, of course, that he does not go away in order to evade his duty and excuse himself from serving his fatherland at the moment when it has need of him. Flight would then be criminal and punishable; that would no longer be withdrawal, but desertion.